WOMEN ON THE EDGE

Forty Three Monologues

by Monique Carmona

Published by Monique Carmona
Santa Monica, CA
www.Monique Carmona.com

Cover Design: Daria Nakelska
Book Layout: Lynnette Rozine Prock

Printed by CreateSpace

©2012

FOREWORD

by Angela Nicholas:
Author of 99 *Film Scenes For Actors,* which ranks as a top 10 best seller on Amazon in "Acting and Auditioning."

A monologue is a personal thing.

I have an early memory of the monologues in this book. A memory of Monique performing them in a class we took, some years ago, with an inspiring teacher, Mark Monroe. Monique would get up to work, announce that she was doing an original piece, and we would all know we were in for a treat. And off she would go — on a defensive rant, or a suffering musing, or a free-associative diatribe, or a masochistic confession. Speaking the unspeakable. Blasting the ego to smithereens. Voicing the absurd. Going on long journeys of tangents and somehow, in an exquisitely circular and human way, finding her way back again. And we'd sit there, wondering what exactly it was we'd just witnessed.

As a pile of words on a page, any one of these pieces might resemble an eccentric ramble towards the Next Big Question, a question that, in each piece, is invariably left unanswered. But as a possibility for redemption, a miniature kabuki representation of the soul's greater struggle, they each offer a golden opportunity – a chance for any actor to hang her singular humanity upon them. They are unspecific enough to embody any bold choice about time, place, people and events, and yet each asks a particular, painful question about the nature of humanity and the multi-layered coping mechanisms we all cling to, to make "sense" of it.

I'm sure I don't have to explain to anyone why this collection is called "*Women on the Edge.*" And we might assume we all know, of course, what "the edge" is but just for a moment: take a breath, leave your mind open, and leap. Could it be the edge of sanity? The edge of salvation? The edge of despair? The edge of enlightenment?

Open this volume, at any page, and try one (or more) of these human conditions on for size. You may find that, after navigating through a seemingly pile of words on a page, you'll have made your way through a emotional morass, into a spiritual epiphany, down a visceral rabbit-hole, and beyond an intellectual looking-glass, to your unique personhood, your unique pain, your unique truth, your unique behavior – all the ingredients of a unique character on a stage.

And now perhaps I've become too esoteric, too far-flung, too cosmic. What I mean to say is this: a monologue is a personal thing. And while the author created these pieces from her very personal journey, her own struggle with the truth of being human, you can come at them from exactly where you are.

You can become intimate with your own humanity, and step into these words like a crazy yellow polka-dot dress. Or a fetching blue scarf. Or a pair of dangerous stilettos. And see how these words make you feel. See how these words make you behave. See how these words make you create. See how these words make you be.

Just take a breath, leave your mind open and leap.

AUTHOR'S NOTES

When I think about the lessons I've learned as a student, an artist, and ultimately a human being, I've come to see that we truly are much more alike than we are different.

Within all of us, there are fundamental needs. I find that when an audience can resonate with their own needs through the work of the actor and through the written word, there can be no greater reward. What is it about an incredible performance? Is it the actor providing a space for the audience to feel the many facets of being alive? I have found this to be a personal truth.

I started writing these pieces from a desire to discover and dive into compelling characters that are flawed, honest and alive. They stand alone as vignettes ready to be imbued and explored...enjoy them. I wrote these monologues for you, not some person you construct or pretend to know. For you.

Utilize your own unique, beautiful resources as you work on these pieces. One of my favorite teachers said to me once, "The thing that is most private and secret to you is the very thing that people want to see most." I believe it, as a student, an artist, and ultimately a human being.

MANY THANKS

There is so much richness right under our noses. I truly feel blessed to be a part of it all. I want to acknowledge all my companions that took this journey with me, your love and talent are forever a gift. I want to acknowledge the characters that stand on the edge with me, fantastic and flawed… and lastly, the ones that take it from the edge, soar and share with the world a bit of their souls.

FOR HEATHER
Always on the edge

WHERE TO FIND WHAT

COMEDY

SERIO-COMEDY

DRAMA

COMEDY

THIS ISN'T DRAMA 101 FOLKS!

Comedy:
An obsessed drama teacher takes her job a little too seriously.

Can I get some Goddamn lights on in here? Please! Okay, thank you. People! People!!! What we are looking at here are some serious organization problems. Right, this show is going up in less than one week. Count them folks, five days. We are talking about a major meltdown with notoriety, popularity and all of the T's you jackasses can come up with. This breaks my heart, however, the Great Oak Tree has been pulled out of the show and we're going to have to replace him with Pezzy the Dope Dealer. Look, I don't need the glares. Go take it to your science teachers, whatever! Either stay on the boat or let go of the rope, because frankly, I don't have the time. Let me make myself perfectly clear. I took this summer job because you retards can't seem to make the grades. I told you all this class could be a cakewalk if you just followed simple directions but apparently you guys just want to act like pansy ass prima donnas. I've been looking and there aren't any Shirley MacLaines in here. You dig? Hey, Sherlock Holmes! You. That's right. (points to her eyeballs) Right Here! Close the book. There isn't anything to figure out. This isn't Social Studies. This, my friend, is the real world. You think Matt Damon made it by studying other subjects in drama class? Do you? All right, there's the bell. Get the hell out of here. Oh, I need the permission slips filled out by your parents no later than Friday. I personally don't agree with the politics behind the third grade, but I don't run this school, I just run this class. Katie, honey, don't forget your lunch box.

FIRST DATE ASSUMPTIONS

Comedy:
An open look at the assumptions we put on people and the pitfalls of stereotyping.

I can't do it. I'm just no good with first dates. I'm too suspect. I went out with that young budding architect last weekend. Yeah, the Scandinavian dreamy one I kept going on about. So, for the first date it's going pretty well. Solid, funny, a bit dry and you know how I love dry. Anyway, I'm totally getting into it and we decide to go back to his place. He pours some wine, shows me a few of his "plans" and then at some point heads to the bathroom and tells me to make myself comfortable. I saunter over to check out his CD's. Well, where do I begin? I was frightened. Everything I was seeing was daunting. I'm thinking the guy obviously has mother issues. He's got every Barry White song ever made so I know there's something going on there. What exactly? I don't know - that he thinks he's a player, maybe? That he IS a player but too obvious a player, which I guess makes him not a player in the truest sense of the word. Let's move on to Barbara Streisand... Barbara Streisand? I thought this guy was in his 30's, not to mention he's probably more fragile than me. Bells are going off. "Get the hell out of here," I'm thinking. I could here him whistling in the bathroom and I'm like, "please don't whistle a musical, please!" I know it's kind of crazy. I had, in less than three minutes run through this man's whole identity profile and assessed the conclusion of a not yet started relationship. I'm not proud. It's like we've become so jaded. I haven't hit thirty and I know by a persons CD collection what I will or will not get out of the experience? "Oh, this guy, total passive aggressive with major penis issues. This one, granola backpacking tree hugger." I mean, who even has CD's anymore anyway? but seriously, It's as if we've all been given too much information. We think we know so much and it's all bull shit... and yet, in a sick sort of way it makes total sense too. Really? Am I only going to marry the man who has my CD collection? Am I looking for my soul mate or my freaking twin? You have to admit though, when my sister found out she was dating an ex con, looking back on it, there in lied the evidence. So anyway, back to the date. He comes out of the bathroom, sits down, sees me holding a CD, which I think was Celtic Flutes or something and says, "You like Celtic? I wouldn't have pegged you as the type. If you want my music it's on my play list, those are my roommates. Yeah, I forgot he had a roommate. So, I've decided from this whole thing to A) relax and B) to never ever date his roommate. Yeah, so I feel pretty good about that decision.

BITTER BRIDESMAID

Comedy:
An obviously frustrated, single bridesmaid tells a scary account of her last friend's wedding.

I have heard of weddings that are over the top but this one just took the cake. Don't presume that I'm just another bitter bridesmaid reaching her thirties projecting her unhappiness onto what others might see as a glorious event. Don't. It was ridiculous! Whatever happened to a priest, some friends, family and a simple "I do"? The bridesmaids were made to feel like we were in Paris about to do our first major catwalk down the runway. Isn't it enough that I flew three thousand miles to get here? No! She had us booked like we were doing a four day gig. I couldn't budge. I can understand her need to have everyone together, you know, to keep things organized, but for Christ's sake, when we got there she made us wear pagers. Hello? I have a phone. I didn't even know they made pagers anymore. Then there was the wonderful experience with the in-laws. The mother in law made Satan look innocent. Look lady, I'm here on vacation, I don't need to hear that I'm nothing but a floozy. Three events were cancelled last minute. The bride's family sold their house to pay for the reception. It just made me nauseous, except for the open bar, which at one point made it all worth it. Apparently, I learned I don't walk slowly enough, my hair just looks better if I completely change it, and I'm not even willing to try to catch a bouquet. Yes, yes, I realize I've become anal, inflexible to other people's needs and would rather spend money on, gee I don't know, a jet plane! I'm trying to recycle my dress but apparently fuchsia and Jennifer don't mix. Paybacks are hell my friend.

HYPNOTIST OR HYPE?

Comedy:
An over-enthused woman chats about her new experience with her Hypnotherapist.

Hey Stranger! So good to see you. You look great. Oh me? Why thank you kindly. I've been seeing this hypno-therapist. She has completely changed my life. In less than three months, I've quit smoking, sugar and sodium! It's like I've had these blinders taken off and I see the world in a whole new light. At first I was afraid, you know, the chance that I might be getting brainwashed or something but after my ninth week, that whole idea just sort of vanished. My relationship with my mother couldn't be better and my boyfriend, well, he has become absolutely fantastic. The sex has reached a whole new level. We're up to four times a day and I get breakfast in bed every morning. The only downfall is that I fall asleep in the middle of the day for about two hours, which can really be a drag when you're working or driving but I've been telling everyone I know about my hypnotist. I feel like I'm on a mission to let everyone know that they should see her. You know, if you look into my eyes like you keep doing, I'm going to hypnotize you. Kidding! I am trained but I don't want to mess with the karma on that one. No thank you! I do feel judged sometimes though, but I think people are just jealous about my success. All you have to do is look at a monitor with these crazy visuals on them for an hour and put these special heated slippers on at the same time and the session is over until next week. Sure, from time to time, I get a glazed look on my face but I figure we're all already sort of hypnotized in a way, if you think about it. (leaning in convincingly) I mean, if I promised you that you could have everything you've ever wanted and all you had to do was wear special slippers and deal with a few side effects, wouldn't you sign up? I'm hypnotizing you again… Psych! Wow, would you look at the time. I have to run. I'm signed up for the L.A marathon. I haven't trained but not to worry, I'm scheduled for five sessions with Sheryl the hypnotist. Here's her card. The first session is free but I'm sure you'll be sold.

HONESTLY BILL

Comedy:
A woman clearly unsatisfied with her own life,
relentlessly takes it out on her husband.

Honestly Bill, I think the last time I saw a smile on
your face was when my mother slipped and almost
broke her hip and don't try to feed me that bull crap
that you were watching Sponge Bob. That's a childish
show Bill, for children. My point? My point is that
you seem unhappy to me lately. You seem miserable,
depressed and quite frankly it's all very pitiful. Look,
I realize how brutal I sound but for God's sake Bill,
I feel like you're punishing me. You used to at least
attempt to be something acceptable. Is that it? Are
you still trying to punish me? You're still mad at me
for that little fling I had. What did I spend over three
thousand dollars and six months of therapy on Bill?
Certainly not an angry, resentful husband. I said I
was sorry. I told you I didn't love him. What more
do you want from me? Why? Why? Why is it so
difficult for you to forgive? When I married you, I
didn't hear anything about "Do you take this woman
only if she's perfect?" If you're looking for perfect, go
to another planet, baby cakes! See, even now you say
nothing. You just sit there with the remote in one
hand and a Snapple in the other and what is it with
the Snapple? Is that your way of saying ,"I'm trendy!
I just turned fifty but I still drink Snapple?" Why do
I even bother? Wait, why do I feel like I'm the asshole

here? Some people might call me mean and nasty but you know what, Bill? I think I'm just stupid to stay. I must be stupid. Why are you laughing, Bill? I don't think that's funny. I suppose you think you've won. You know what you can do with that Snapple, Bill? I have to go, I'm late for therapy.

No One's Home... Leave A Message

Comedy:
A neurotic woman identifies the trappings of giving too much energy and time to her answering machine.

I need help. I was putting a new message into my voice mail, you know, the basic "leave a message and I'll call you back" thing. I realized after spending over fifteen minutes doing this that I had a bit of a problem. I know everybody wants to leave a cute, charming-whatever-impression on their callers but I think I set a whole new record. I literally witnessed all the people I think I want to be. It was, well, disturbing. At one point I almost had a reenactment of that movie Sybil going on. Sure, some were pretty savvy but anyone listening in would have seen there was way too much time going into the whole situation. Let's see, there was reserved and mysterious me, thought provoking with a hint of sage-like wisdom and basically a slough of bad attempts of who I could be. Somewhere in between the eighth and ninth try, it hit me how lonely I must be that I have to entertain myself with this nonsense. I spent a good half hour tracking the neurosis behind it all. I'm aware it's odd times for a lot of people right now, but its shit like this that makes me wonder. Are we all this freaky? Nobody is really going to give a crap about what I'm saying. That's what I'm really afraid of. I'm afraid no one gives a crap. (phone rings) Oh, excuse me, I should take this call.

I HAVE EXQUISITE BUNS

Comedy:
A woman becomes overtly smitten with a houseguest and attempts to convince him, in any way possible, not to leave.

I don't think it's a smart idea for you to leave right now. As a matter of fact, the more I think about it, it's downright ridiculous. Suicidal, even. I mean, what's the point of running after a woman when all she cares about are stupid things like security, wealth and power? It's raining. The last time it rained like this something unspeakable happened. If you make yourself comfortable, I'm sure you will come to your senses and see that she was just using you. I know you don't think you have security, wealth or power, but I saw it in her eyes, like a wolf, she was using you. Did you know I'm quite proficient when it comes to cooking? I also scored incredibly high on both the emotional and intellectual IQ tests. I'm so sorry you couldn't find your keys. I would let you borrow my vehicle if I had one. You could get right in and tell her what's what. Boy, that woman couldn't see the best thing of her life if it were crawling right in her ear. You know, now that I've got you here for a few moments, I thought maybe we could discuss how you feel about children and horses. I imagine you to be quite the animal lover. You seem as if you're bothered in some way. If you just surrender to the storm… Of course, I'm speaking both metaphorically and literally. If you just surrender to the storm, I'm sure you'll realize she's just a tramp. Oh, no, I said you'll realize how damp it is out there. So… here we are. I'm sure those keys will show up in a perfect, timely manner. Everything around here always seems like it does. For example, the day we met, perfect timely manner. Had you come only one day sooner, I would have still been on my trip in South America rescuing those poor, helpless bobcats. (she pulls out a tray of buns) Would you care for a bun? I have exquisite buns.

WHAT A JOKE!

Comedy:
An unresolved women dealing with a lingering lover desperately questions why men and woman have difficulties in relationships.

What a joke. I can't believe he'd come crawling back to me after he left me for that hooker. I know she's a secretary, it just feels right to call her a hooker, okay? This whole thing has gotten so confusing with him. I'm just totally screwed up about men. It's like God is just playing this huge practical joke on us all, like it's a big game. I can just see him with the scoreboard, you know? By the way, Jim just scored ten bonus points for the male species and for that I'm not proud. What? You don't think it's crazy the way people handle relationships? We act like animals when it comes to relationships. The only difference is they're fighting over the trees and bushes and we're fighting over the cars and houses. Seriously, I give up. Oh yeah, and then the women end up being the bitches if anything isn't "groovy." I couldn't sleep at all last night. I just kept trying to figure it all out. (trying to convince) I came up with this idea! It's a pretty good idea. See I went all the way back! Okay, check it out, God and Adam are playing this intense game of golf. Well, Adam's taking it very seriously and well, God being God and all, he lets Adam win. But see, Adam starts getting cocky with God, so God says "Son, you think you have attitude... let me show you something with real attitude," and low and behold, there was Eve. (very proud of herself) So you see, it's been a battle from the get-go. Don't get me wrong, I'm not putting women down. I think we are what make this planet so beautiful. It's all too much. If I had any dignity left, I'd be a real woman and go in that room right now and tell him "thanks, but no thanks." I'd waltz my sweet ass in MY bedroom and stand on these two beautiful feet and tell that no good for nothing. Yeah! I'm going to go in there right now!!! I'm going to go in there right now and tell him. That his breakfast is ready? (confused) Oh, sweet Jesus.

JETHROW ON DEATH ROW

Comedy:

A woman in need of love attempts to explain her fondness for a death row inmate to a support group.

I have a fascination for death row inmates. I know that must sound morbid but I really think it's just my fear of commitment and my love for Susan Sarandon. You know, Susan, she was in that "Dead Man Walking." Let's see, it started about two years ago. Jethrow and I started corresponding out of Pensacola State Prison. Oh, he is so lovely. He adores animals and children so much. Sometimes, he says he adores them too much. He says that's what got him behind bars… that and just an inconvenient run-in with a real mean teacher who was acting up with his cousin. Oh and there's the thing with the cats. Anyhow, he's working on his first book "Recipes from the Penthouse." There are all these wonderful dishes that originally start as junk and he literally transforms them. He's been on Oprah, not once but twice! Some special she was doing. I'm not sure on what exactly but Oprah's huge. To top it off, he's planning on running for State Congress in three years. I love a man with ambition. My Aunt Colleen said he is just taking advantage of my condition. I have a little problem sometimes, is all, thinking clearly, but that's just cause of my accident with a school bus, but I really have no condition to speak of (starts twitching and mumbling) No condition, condition, condition, (spelling it out) C O N D I T I O N. (composing herself) I've never had such an exciting affair before in my life. He writes every day and he says, although he's not physically with me, he is spiritually with me all the time. That's fine. I think the fact that they're going to fry him only reaffirms my draw to men that I can not truly commit to. I'm trying to talk my friend Rebecka into meeting his "neighbor." Becky isn't usually into three time sex offenders but I know that as soon as she finds out he writes poetry, makes a mean lasagna land and goes to church regularly, she'll be making that trip with me to Pensacola. You all should not judge if you haven't walked in Jethrow's footsteps. Really, you shouldn't.

FORTUNE COOKIE

Comedy:

An overworked woman seeks consolation in an undependable fortune cookie.

I feel so ripped off. I'm at this oriental restaurant last week with some co-workers enjoying a quick meal, and after lunch, we all get our ritualistic fortune cookie. "Great," I think to myself. "An opportunity for some optimistic one liner to get me through my work week." Fortune cookie. For–tune-cook-ie. Cookie with a fortune. What does mine say? My fortune cookie says… "Be very cautious in life with untrustworthy friends. Danger is everywhere!" Really? "Be cautious in life with untrustworthy friends?" I'm wondering, is this supposed to bring me comfort? Joy? Is this honestly supposed to cut it? I pay for a good meal. I wait patiently, for what in my eyes is a very short version of a tarot card reading. I'm actually excited about this whole damn thing! Cautious? Untrustworthy? I read that somewhere in last month's Cosmo. I really do not need to hear it again. Then, of course, I check with everyone at the table. "Money is everywhere in your near future." "Wisdom and integrity bring you constant insight." "You are irresistible to all of the opposite sex." That last one just did it. Obviously, I refused to share mine. These could be the untrustworthy friends my fortune cookie was talking about. Sad, I know. Even sadder is my faith in the magic of cookies. See, when I was in high school, I worked at a Chinese restaurant and a big part of my innocence was taken away when I would spend up to an hour every shift cracking fortune cookies open. Like clockwork, every four to five would be repeats. But Never in all that time did I ever encounter any crap about shooting your friends or locking yourself up for the weekend to stay out of trouble. I guess the other night was just a reminder of what I already knew. Sometimes, you may get lucky four times in a row and it may not mean anything. Sometimes, you do not get lucky four times in a row and that may not mean anything either. Sometimes, you should just trade cookies.

THE SIDE EFFECTS FROM HOLDING OFF

Comedy:
A woman processes her journey through a sexless time in her life.

Can I talk to you about sex? Sure I could just beat around the bush, or I could just get honest about the whole thing, try to find some sense of relief in hearing myself analyze the situation... some sense that I'm smart and witty and not just lonely and horny. God, I hate that word, horny. Horny. Oohh, it just conjures up visions of warts and toads. Not sexy. Sexy, sex, right! That was my point. Sex, or lack thereof, which in my case, is the latter of the two. It's firstly, embarrassing that I sound like some sort of Ann Landers fan that never got a reply and secondly, shocking that someone with my Je ne sais quoi... striking beauty, could have managed to somehow pigeon-hole herself into being a practical virgin. I thought I would wait until Mr. right came knocking on my uterus and now I'm to the point where I'm practically making drive-bys at the local high school. Ok, so I'm exaggerating. There was the long distance thing I was doing for a while. I mean, what was that anyway, right? Okay, so there was the one time with phone sex but I saw no penis, I held no flesh. I mean there are 100, 000 available men in the state of California and I've got to pay Verizon five cents a minute, "not including weekends" to get off? My luck, I'll find out the operator was in on the whole thing and we had a threesome, whoo-hoo! I'll find out when I get the bill and get charged for the back to back orgasms! You know how they say we renew our chromosomes every five years? You'd like to think a woman could go full circle with her virginity. That's the least she should get for not giving it up to any Tom, Dick or Harry. A virginity badge of some sort, something, a head board with zero notches on it. Trust me, I haven't heard my headboard in a while. Originally, this whole thing started so that frivolous sex or meaningful, for that matter, wouldn't get in the way of the relationship. I figured it wasn't worth it if I wanted to bail before the sun came up because the actual thought of being with one another was worse than putting a fork in my neck. I want to roll over and know everything is revered, appreciated, and safe and then I think 'this isn't the Walton's honey! This is the real world!' but then I don't want to be an Ice Queen either. I know all about my past and how I try to protect myself and not get close. I'm over it. It's tired. I already read the book on that. What I would give to ride on a carpet of pleasure and no regret. There's an idea! I'm going to take myself off this hamster wheel I've put myself on, I'm going to press stop on this tape recorder that's playing the same damn tune called the drama of my life and I'm going to go get laid. Oh God, I hate that word too. I'm going to… undulate on the opposite sex. That's better! I like the way that sounds. Thank you so much. You are such a good listener. Do you have any condoms? Don't worry, I'm not gonna do anything stupid. I realize I've created some story that it should look a certain way. I had hope for a noble, nurturing relationship and in fact that may happen but it starts with my loosening up and having a better connection to healthy fornication. Who knows? This date I have on Friday night may just be the right combo of a healthy mind, a healthy heart and a very, very healthy penis. Penis, now there's a word I can resonate with. Penis.

ARMED AND READY

Comedy:

A young woman submerged in a gang life style tries convincing her friend how smart and together she is.

Pistol whipping. You know, pistol whipping! You get the back of the gun and you smack the mother fucker's face. It's a big insult 'cause you could kill them, you know, cause you're holding the gun and everything, but you want to just bitch slap them with your metal. My old man told me these crazy war stories about guns. Crazy "Apocalypse Now" stories and he was always the star. Yeah, I know he's a mechanic. You don't think I know what my old man does for a living? Do you see eyes in my head? I'm talking about back in the day. He was in the military before he went AWOL. It's this place for special genius officers. That's when the gun stories happened. My old man told me I've had a gun since day one. Since the day I was born, I had one under my crib. He said you never can be too careful. Oh, he's real careful, though. He's very careful who he shows his gun collection to. Real careful who he buys from, real careful who he sells to. You know, overall very careful. I've only ever shot someone once. He was in my place uninvited, thief, maybe even a rapist, but I wasn't gonna find out, hell na. My old man said he was real proud of me but I think it shocked him or something because for like a month my guns were missing and all he wanted to do with me was go shopping and shit. (shows off her threads) Yeah, the whole outfit, you like it? Dude, that gun you got there is just way too big. Who do you think you are? Clint Eastwood? This isn't The Good, Bad and the Ugly! You need a gun that's personalized, customized, kinda like a bowling ball but a lot more powerful. (sees the gun is pointing at her) That shit better be on safety lock! Do I look like an amateur to you?

WHOLLY MIRED

Comedy:
Exhausted by the insanity of her day-to-day encounters, this trendy, passionate woman shares her latest dramas at the local Whole Food Market.

All right my friend, picture this... I'm in Whole Foods, just minding my own business, looking for some organic gummy bears, when what do I see? What do I see with these two eyes? A baby. Get this, no more than a blob of a being, naked, lying on the conveyer belt, absolutely naked. No! He wasn't alone. Jesus, could you just let me tell you the story? Thank you! Anyway, his mother, if that's what you want to call her, is changing his or her diaper, actually using the register as some make-shift baby station. I was shocked. I needn't tell you what I saw. Yes. I saw and smelled. Yes, it's sad but true. Well, I reported it immediately to the manager. I've had indigestion from the whole ordeal for five hours now. Oh, you should have seen the look on the baby's face. Now that I think about it, it was definitely a man-child. He looked as if he were King Tut, just lying there with that shit eating grin on his face. At one point he looked right in my eyes and in that moment, I knew that he knew that I knew that he knew. It was creepy. What kind of rearing is this? I mean, if you can just take a dump on register five when you're not even old enough to speak, what advantages do you think you'll be taking by the time you're say eight or nine?

I just used the word dump. This entire day has been tragically upsetting. The manager asks the mother real PC like, why she had not used the rest room. Apparently, smokers had been in the vicinity and she didn't want to disturb or harm the baby in any way. HELLO? Harm the baby? I don't think I'll ever be able to shop at my favorite store again. I'll have visions of number two engrained in my head any time I purchase anything. I'll have to start shopping on-line just not to get queasy and she's worried about King Tut inhaling what she thinks could have been smoke. The irony of this woman. I really feel like something should be done. I should do some picketing. "If you want to stay alive, wouldn't put my food on register five." You know, something that leaves them questioning, something live and punchy. You think I'm kidding? Did you know that feces are poisonous? I'm not just bitching here because I couldn't find my stupid gummy bears. Oh and just for the record, I went into that bathroom... fresher than a summer breeze, thank you. I think this whole trend with natural living has just become some scapegoat for anyone to do anything they damn well please. Are you still getting those headaches after you see me? I think that is so strange. Maybe it's my perfume. Have you had your asbestos levels checked? What? It worries me that you may be living in a lead laden home and you give me this look like you're really not that interested. Like I'm being dramatic. (pulls out a baggie) Want some dried papaya?

BLIND DATE ANYONE?

Comedy:
A woman, desperate for love, completely and shamelessly puts herself out there as she dominates her blind date.

This place is really cool. Yeah, I couldn't have picked a better place for a blind date. Is this something you do all the time? Oh, no of coarse not. Me? Nope. This is my first. I'm lying. There was a kid my mom set me up with when I was fifteen. I took one look at this guy and thought man, my mom either really hates me or just does not find her little girl attractive at all. He was a sweet guy though, but other than that, nope. So, this is really nice here. Busy place, huh? I mean the waitress must really want us to get to know each other because she has just dis-a-peared. Have you been here before? Really, so this where you bring all your victims? Kidding. I kid when I get nervous. And well, my sister didn't tell me you were so cute. Do you think I'm cute? Please don't answer that. That was just me trying to be manipulative. Me trying to "figure you out" but I like some things to be mysterious. I guess that's why I said yes to the blind thing. Blind thing, that sounds so dark, like you're going to poke my eyes out or something. Like I was saying, I don't want to start this relationship, or any relationship for that matter, like all my others, always trying to compete. Always having to judge one another in order to feel like I'm in control. Nope. Not any more. Not me. I have to tell you, I read the most phenomenal book last week and I'm not exaggerating when I say, I put the book down and BOOM the phone rang. It was my sister setting me up on this very date. This very special engagement. Weird ha? So Richard, do you like Rich? Or Richard? What does everybody call you? Dick? Really? My sister said it was Richard. Oh, right that is a nickname for Richard isn't it? Okay! Well, where was I? So, Dick, did I tell you how, (she stops herself) would you mind if I called you something else, something other than the male reproductive organ? Anything? I am not trying to be offensive but who are we kidding? Every time that word is tossed around, anyone within ear shot... Well, let's just say it might not be too appetizing. (silence) I really hope you don't mistake my passion for life for unnecessary drama or obsessive neurotic behavior because let me tell you, I am a passionate woman Richard. P a s s i o n a t e. This place is really nice.

WHAT DO I HAVE TO DO?

Comedy:
A disgruntled actress complains about the irony of "making it" and the levels to which one will go.

Did you hear about the woman who robbed an ATM machine and got away with the money until they found the footage of her a week later at the very same ATM? She was applying lip liner in the mirror. You know the one that's got the camera behind it. The story goes she was a struggling actress and tried saying that stealing was a tool for her craft and she had an upcoming role where she was a thief. She said her intentions were all good and that she works best when she becomes the character. Would you give me a break? I know we're all trying to be found and you never know who you're going to bump into but "HELLO!" Primping at the same bank you're robbing? I bet this chick is going to get exactly what she wants from this whole thing. Publicity, exposure that will mean an upgrade to a better agency. I can see a best seller "I did it all for love." She'll say the torment of being a starving actress drove her to temporary insanity. All the stolen money went to funding the end of crack houses and black market babies. I know I sound like a jealous, disgruntled actress but what do I have to do? Hijack a plane to get a movie of the week? Since I was a kid, my favorite show has been Saturday Night Live. I've always wanted to be a part of that cast and now apparently if you're caught shoplifting or blowing a president you get to be the guest star. I guess there's no business like show business. What were we talking about? Oh, yeah right, you were saying you are in it for the pure craft, yeah, me too. I mean, what else is there?

OPEN YOUR EYES!

Comedy:
A paranoid woman tries to convince her roommate that the DMV is an undercover front for a governmental scam. Everywhere this woman looks, she sees conspiracy.

I was at the DMV of all places and that's when it hit me! The car! The car! Jesus Christ. I was just trying to get my license renewed. I have a pretty clean record, for the most part. I, like millions of other Americans, have to go to this place of limbo and be under the thumb of yet another Big Brother organization. I mean, isn't it enough that we are constantly being brainwashed? Constantly being governed like a bunch of guinea pigs? No. I have to get hit by some underpaid, over-pumped robot of a person, who I'm sure was hired by the DMV to take down a certain number of innocent bystanders of life. (shocked) What? What am I saying? Are you seriously kidding with me right now? Didn't you hear a word I just said? What I'm saying is that there's a manipulation going on here, Peter, a shakedown, a conspiracy of sorts going on. My God, man! Open your eyes! Let's try this again, shall we? I'll speak slowly and clear. (checking over her shoulder) I was hit by a moving ve-hic-le. I was unable to get my license renewed, rushed to the hospital in some pathetic attempt to act like they cared. Now, I have to wait another six weeks for another chance. Now, I look like the bad guy, the vagrant who can't seem to make simple things happen. I'm attending a meeting tonight with seventeen other people who know what I'm talking about here, Peter. It's always the same model car in several different locations, always on weekdays, not counting holidays. What other kinds of assassins take holidays off? I think I'm just scratching the surface here. I have reasons to believe this is just a smaller vein going into an entire body of destruction, Peter. (starting to leave) I'm going to need to borrow a few things from you and ask that you keep everything we've spoken about here confidential. Did you read in the paper about the woman who caught on fire outside the post office? Spontaneous combustion my ass! (suspiciously) Why are you looking at me like that, Peter?

THE TWISTS OF HIGH SCHOOL

Comedy:
A woman candidly recalls the growing pains of a high school crush... with the same sex.

I remember details. Her name was Leslie Parker. She was a blonde, which for the life of me I can't figure out why I was so drawn to her. Blondes don't normally do anything for me. Wait a second, girls didn't normally do anything for me either, which brings me to my point. I was fifteen, maybe sixteen. I remember being as hetero as it gets. I wasn't exactly on top of the world with the boys in school but I knew I liked guys. Here I am, walking to class and I take a look at her from across the hall. I get this flutter in my belly through my legs and I stop dead in my tracks. Silently shocked, I simultaneously get aroused and go into a major panic attack. Could I be the first lesbian at Jefferson High? Jesus Christ! I lost it. No one must know. OH my God. I looked at a woman and got a twitch, a mmmm, a moment of ecstasy that would usually be brought on by a Jim, a Bobby, or a Henry. Not a Jennifer. I felt like I was walking to class butt naked. There we were in the locker room. I felt like I should warn the girls that there was a peeping Tom present or should I say peeping Jane. "Hey Darcy, how's it going? Could you cover up? I'm about to reach out and see what it feels like to touch your breasts." I definitely would not be making it on the cheerleading team. Wrestling was always an option. I was the right size. I thought I had totally lost my mind. Well, that was in the ninth grade and by the time I was a junior, I was in full bloom with the boys. I decided to sweep the whole lesbian episode under the rug. Now that I'm older, or as I like to put it, wiser, I look back and giggle. I still look at women but I know it's natural. Look, I happen to undoubtedly adore men. There's been times though, after a real hard break up with a man, some daunting interlude with a man- boy or just a real tired ass date, I get to wondering what that Leslie is up to these days. Like I said, I love men. It's just sometimes I probably love them a little too much.

Roller Derby Chick

Comedy:

A spacey, eccentric, young woman shares her unfiltered thoughts about the adventures of her life.

Let's see… I guess the weirdest thing I ever did was the time I poured hot wax all over the bottom half of my body. I wanted to see if I could step out of it, put it back together again and use it for an art exhibit going on at the high school gymnasium. I wanted to play ZZ Top's "She's Got Leg's." I wanted to hook up some Christmas light that could blink to the beat of the music. It would have been super cool and would have totally blown everyone away except for the fact that it was summer school. It was out of control hot in the gym so it was more like "She's got crap and she knows how to do that." One time I made a giant skittle ball out of a shit load of skittles, now that was a true success. I ate off of it for an entire week. It was like the big gobstopper out of the movie "Charlie and the Chocolate Factory." That's kind of like science and art… melting stuff. I was voted most original in my high school, which basically means weird. It's all the same to me. Original, weird, different, special and then there's just boring, plain, common. Personally, I never want to be any of those things. (contemplates) If I could go to the moon right this second, I would get in a rocket right now, dirty hair and all. I would request that I would get to wear my roller skates so that I would be the first roller derby chick ever to stare back at this wacky planet earth. I would ask if I could do karaoke. I'd sing Patsy Kline's "Crazy." I know how far out that sounds, really, I do. If I could go to the moon, I don't see why I couldn't skate and sing a little too. (starts singing) "Crazy, crazy for feeling so lonely... "

SERIO-COMEDY

You Don't Deserve This

Serio-Comedy:
After demanding that her unfaithful lover move out, a woman returns home to find that he wants to try and save the relationship.

I think the worst thing next to death, by my darkest conceivable nightmare, is having to see your face when I walk through this door after I have clearly told you I want you and all your things out of my life for the last time. Let me guess, you thought we could talk, maybe even grow from this whole thing. WRONG! I was at work today thinking about all the different kinds of footwear I could kick you with, while you were blindfolded and naked. I don't think that's something we can work on, honey. I don't see that as a healthy relationship thought. I know I'm not attractive when I think these things and I know that wouldn't feel good if I actually followed through, so what I suggest is that you save all the explanations, stories and wonderful antidotes for the lucky ducky I found you in bed with. IN MY BED! You unbelievably selfish bastard. What gets me is that now I get to spend the next six months proving to myself that your actions say nothing about my worth. The whole thing didn't mean anything. It was what it was and life goes on, c'est la vie!! Maybe I'll see I'm actually responsible for the things that happen in my life and I actually manifested a man who couldn't keep his dick in his pants while I was away for two weeks. You know what? I am so hurt I could spit. I don't understand you. I don't understand myself. I don't even understand what I'm supposed to understand. I just know that I did not want this to turn out this way. I don't want to think that I'm not ready to be loved or love because of what I didn't get from my parents and that everyone I date is just some weird opportunity to re-meet and re-do the way I operate. I'm tired of everyone being another lesson. I just want. Forget it. You don't deserve this conversation. You don't get another breath of mine. Get Out.

CRAZY

Serio-Comedy:
A woman caught up in the karaoke scene and a dysfunctional relationship goes over the events leading up to a ridiculous, horrifying evening. Here we see a woman side stepping her dreams and satisfying herself with one of the 21st century wonders: Karaoke.

There's this karaoke bar I used to go to with a bunch of friends back when I worked with Harold. Every Tuesday night like clock work, we'd head down there. After about three captain and cokes, I'd be warmed up and a little less shy and I'd sing like a bird. Oh, I wouldn't say it if it weren't true. I'm not too good at too many things but singing, well, I could hum a tune or two. Harold never came down on Tuesdays. That was his poker night with the crew of guys from the garage. I'd always fantasized about him walking in and I'd be singing as sweet as a dove and he'd walk up to me and ask me to move to Nashville with him. But who was I to come between a man and his poker game? They were all heavy drinkers and he wouldn't usually come home until well after 4:00 a.m. There was always some petty ass rumor goin' round the diner that someone was sleeping with someone or some stupid crap like that. Anyways, Max and I had been doin' some pretty hot stuff at karaoke, duets and some real terrific numbers. He was working his way through college getting his bachelor's degree in sociology. He was quite a looker and real easy to talk to, and from time to time, after a couple of drinks, I'd get to wondering about Max and me making a different kind of music together. To tell you the truth, now looking back, I wish I had done something with him but I never did. Since high school I was a fool in love, in love with Harold. I saw somethin' special in that man and even though we'd had our rough times, I knew he was a passionate soulful person. That was until last Tuesday when Harold heard that Max and I had been sleeping together after karaoke. I was up solo doing Patsy Cline and in walks Harold. I was already so high from singin'. I just went right into my vision of us moving away together. I never even got to speak. To say what he had heard was a lie. He dragged me off stage by my hair and made me sit on Max's lap. Nobody could do anything on account of Harold's gun. Then he made me sing into the microphone the rest of the Patsy Cline song to Max with the barrel of the gun to Max's forehead. I saw that passion at the end of his fingertips and he was just waiting for the end of the song to do something. (completely mystified) Someone must have been watching over me that night, because somehow, in the middle of all the chaos, the power went out. No Patsy. No microphone. No lights. In a flash, I knocked the gun away from Max's head and Harold fired and shot the teleprompter. The next thing I knew, he was thrown down and the gun was knocked out of his hand. (takes a while thinking) It's not a good feeling thinking about the man you love turning into a monster. Turning on the only thing that truly loved him. It's all been a big blur. You think you know a few things in life, just a few. Something like that happens, and you realize you don't know nothin'.

BI-POLAR OR JUST HUMAN?

Serio-Comedy:
A woman deals with internal struggles of living with extreme ranges of emotion during very commercialized times.

Sometimes, as I'm waking up I'll look out my window and hope I don't have that empty feeling in the pit of my stomach. I see that I have been given another chance. The slate could be wiped clean and I could recreate myself as I rise from my slumber. These are all the things I think. These are all the things I cognitively run through as I roll over and watch the print of my out of season, fall collection sheets come into focus. I roll over in hopes of waking again without the drama, with the freshness of an Irish Spring commercial. The empty feeling of a bad breakup, maybe even a death in the family is ever present. Being the analytical brainchild I like to hide behind, I go over the many possibilities, angles and reasons for this affair with disaster I have when I rise. A child of God who feels left behind maybe? An hour goes by and I can't share with anyone how paralyzed I feel by my own dismay. Perhaps I'm just exhausted from being so "on" the night before, and the night before that and so far back I can't even fucking remember. "It's not easy being cheesy!" They couldn't have said that better. I'm not what I would consider a split, although, I have visited The North and South Pole in a twenty-four hour period many times. I do well when I'm happy. It feels right. The darkness is filled with light and I can very well break any amount of ice. I guess that's why I feel so crushed when I wake up and don't know why I'm here. I know this shit I'm swimming around in isn't exactly the stuff you take to cocktail parties. Does anyone really want to talk about it? I don't. There are some real dramas going on in my hour or two of reluctance. Babies dying, fires burning down two-hundred-year-old trees like a marathon runner going toward her victory, you name it, it's happening. So, what gives? Who knows, maybe even though I'm an individual lying in my bed thinking about how inconsequential my despair might be, maybe I'm like an eyelash in this body of the world and, from time to time, I can't help but feel what's going on with the rest of me…maybe I should just get up while I can. Maybe I should start with changing these sheets.

Be Careful What You Ask For

Serio-Comedy:
A desperate woman seeks to find resolution with an abrupt break up.

What do want me to say? That we met at a funeral and I should have known that that was not a good sign? OK, so it's not a good sign when you're shaking hands, meeting your new love interest over someone's dead body. I'm usually so open to these kinds of omens but quite frankly, the whole thing was weird. His toothbrush was black. I don't think that's right! I should have seen this coming a mile away. No, all I saw was this shy, beautiful, sensitive, mysterious man. Our first date, a man died at the table next to us. So what, the guy was old. Come-on! First date? Man down? Hello! Noooo, all I saw was Michael, the hero performing C.P.R, "Oh, a certified man!" The guy could have had three black crows flying around his head, I wouldn't have noticed. What ever happened to meeting safe, normal men? I'm really trying not to beat myself up here but after the way we broke up, it's like I was cursed or something. I've never been too superstitious but for Christ's sake, we met at a cemetery. That's worse than a singles bar, right? Where do you go from there? I feel like shit. I don't want to do this anymore. Play this fantasy, fulfill-my-needs crap. I don't want everyone to know how I'm feeling. Can't I keep that? God knows he took my dignity and my Ouija-board… it's just disturbing on so many levels. Have I become a cynical old hag? The soul's a tricky thing or maybe it's the only thing that's not playing tricks. It's the mind I need to watch. You want to know the truth? While I was in this pseudo, forced relationship with a half dead person, I got on my hands and knees and prayed that I might be relieved of my worst pain, loneliness. There, I said it, loneliness. It was that same night that he came and told me it was over. I haven't seen him since, like he never even existed. Be careful what you ask for, you might just get it and have to trust in something.

GALLERY FANTASIES

Serio-comedy;
A woman with too much time on her hands at work seduces her partner with a fantasy she had on the clock.

I was at the gallery today and everyone was gone. They all had meetings, dates, whatever it is they do. I thought about you and I thought of all the pieces we have in the back. You know the Fred Zuckerman collection. The ones with the velvet and handles. I thought of how I wanted you to come into the gallery and act like you didn't know me. I'd show you the pieces and talk about the artist's background and you'd stop and tell me how much you liked this or that particular piece. We'd start touching and kissing and you'd just take me right there in the gallery. Then, my boss would come back from lunch and we'd get off together just as he walked in the front door. And as we heard him walking toward the back, I'd pull my skirt down and you would zip your pants up, just in time for you to say hello to him completely straight faced. You'd walk me to the front and tell me you'd meet me for dinner later. Then, I'd look at my boss and he'd tell me what a great job I was doing at the gallery. But they came back early from lunch and you didn't come by... so. You know, I think we have a couple more days before they change the exhibit. I'd love to see the look on his silly little face.

Don't Call My Mother Fat!

Serio-Comedy:
After having an emotional breakdown, a woman sees the benefit of letting it all out.

Look, I'm sorry I hung the phone up on you last night, I really am. It was inappropriate and childish of me and I hope you can just try and understand that I'm not perfect. You know, like remember the time you called my mother fat by accident or the time you forgot to pick me up from the airport? It's kind of one of those things that after you do it, you realize how much it could hurt someone or how much that person is left feeling totally, utterly unappreciated. I hung up and I just sat there looking at the phone wondering why I would do that to someone I love. I am angry Ted. I'm not going to lie to you. Last night I almost fought with the security guard at Ralph's because he wouldn't let me out the door that was obviously capable of opening. I almost physically assaulted an armed man. They escorted me out. I stood in the middle of the parking lot screaming, just screaming, screaming because I hung up the phone, screaming because you called my mother fat and because of all the other things I just let go by the wayside because… because why Ted? Because I don't make a fuss. Because I have to make sure everything is okay. I don't think I've ever screamed like that in my entire life. Maybe that's why I hung up, because the only other option was to scream into the phone and then you might leave me. Maybe it would have woken you up. You know, really, we've both been asleep. I'm not allowed back to that Ralph's or any other Ralph's for that matter but it felt good afterwards, it felt damn good. So you can sit there all night and sulk because I stood up for once in my life, you can leave, or you can slowly try to wake up with me, because from time to time, if you get to be an insensitive human being who isn't perfect, then from time to time, you might just find me crying, hysterically laughing, dancing naked in the kitchen or whatever the hell I feel like doing. And by the way, don't you ever call my mother fat again.

I WAS EVERYTHING

Serio-Comedy:

A woman experiences amnesia in a local supermarket and sees the different possibilities in forgetting everything from her past.

So there I was, standing in the middle of the supermarket, completely blank, complete memory loss. Nothing. I didn't know who I was, didn't know what I was doing. I didn't know anything, except that I was in a bit of a predicament. So, you look to the obvious. What I had in my basket, rubber gloves, Elmer's Glue, can of cream of corn, diapers. DIAPERS? I didn't feel like a mother. I felt like an alien, but not a mother. I wanted to take a moment with myself before screaming for help. I figured I might look a bit freakish asking someone who I was, and then suddenly getting it all together and remembering everything, only to look like some total drug addict. Well, at least I know I'm neurotic no matter what my name is - definitely neurotic. The oddest thing happened. I started to feel completely excited, elated actually, at the thought of not knowing anything about myself. No past. No track record. I wanted to see if I could look at things in a new light to see what I felt like I liked. Was I a PB and J kind of gal? Did I eat meat? Did I want to eat meat? Did I win the approval of my peers? Was I living happily? I started crying out of the sheer joy of the whole situation. I felt like a reborn soul, carefree. I was given another chance.

But wait! Diapers? It was all too much. I started hyperventilating and that's when you walked up. Am I asthmatic? Don't answer that, please. It's strange, the whole thing... and then you just showed up and shined the light of reality on me like I was lead in *A Chorus Line*. The doctors say it's pretty common. (reminiscing the taste of freedom) It was... for a brief moment, I was everything. (laughing at herself) Can you believe that whole time I had someone else's shopping basket?

MISTER OR MISTRESS?

Serio-Comedy:
An inquisitive, concerned roommate stumbles across some theories to bite into that deal with men, women and power.

I was reading an article at the supermarket about some celebrity who got caught with a mistress he'd had for over five years. Funny thing was, that the focus wasn't even on the guy, it was on this woman who was labeled a "home wrecker," "tramp," you name it, they labeled her! "MISTRESS" in all capitals. It was emblazoned in my mind for the rest of the day. Then I started thinking, "What if it were the other way around?" I mean, if it were a married woman with the unmarried man? What would you call him? What would his label be? What do you call a male version of a mistress? Then it hit me! The male version of a mistress is a MISTER! That's when I got real freaked out because it dawned on me that we were screwed from the get-go. The language is already set up to protect the man. I just pictured all the misters I know, all the misters across the nation just being "mister this" or "mister that." I honestly don't think it's fair. Sure, it might just be a linguistic thing, but okay try this on. "Hi, nice to meet you. My name is Mistress Johnson." NO! That doesn't go over too well. I get a rock thrown at me or make a cover of some cheap newspaper. But Mister Johnson walks away without a scratch. I mean, think about it. The whole thing is creepy. What do you call a scag bitch that cheats with your husband? Mistress, we are agreed on that, right? So what is the male equivalent of that? Mister? I'm not saying I'm going to change the world with my news flash. It's just something to think about the next time you leave it up to one gender. It's like it's too easy for them or something. There isn't even a name for men that cheat. It's like what, a birth right? I don't know. Call me crazy. (trying to calm down) I think I just need to chill. Oh, Mister Perkins called for you while you were gone. He said now would be a good time for you to pick up the supplies you needed. His family is out of town and things are less hectic. If I were you, I'd have him drop them by here. I'm just sayin'.

WHERE DO I BEGIN?

Serio-Comedy:
A first time session with a therapist reveals the intense, sometimes comical experiences of being related to an addict.

What? Do I have any phobias? No, not really. Well, I guess you could say I have a phobia of sorts about projectors. You know the kind where you watch home movies and slides and things. It started when I was about twelve years old living in Miami. I was going with my mom every week to visit my brother Tom in some drug rehab place. They would stick me in this room for what seemed like a hell of a long time. I'd have to watch this projector with shot after shot of junkies and the way they used. I may as well have been abducted by aliens because some of the shit I saw was just wrong. "This is a cocaine user after three years," and then they'd show a shot of a sixty percent deteriorated nose. How they got some of these camera angles is still a mystery to me. Tracks, scars, bruises, free-base, I knew more about their side effects than I did about my homework! More about barbiturates than Barbie dolls. Hey, but it's therapy right? I mean, who were these people? "Let's stick her in a little room and scare the fuck out of her!" I felt like I was the only person in this tiny dark room with this enormous projector remote in my own little hand. I'd just sit watching picture after picture of soulless cadavers with half eaten noses. On a lighter note, one time, we were doing this support circle thing. My mom, my clean brother, Eric, and myself were listening to everybody's stories. There weren't too many dads there, not mine anyways. Anyhow, so everyone's going around the circle and this kid stands up to state his name and drug of choice. He's got that real southern drawl, chewing dip, cap, well mannered, you know the whole bit. "Hi, my name is Albi and my drug of choice is gas-O-line." He says and sits back down. Before anyone could even contemplate some sixteen year old kid hovering over a gas tank inhaling to get high, he stands back up real quickly and says, "Oh, I'm sorry, that's regular." Regular? It was just so crazy. I guess it's kind of sad. It seemed funny at the time but not so much here talking to you. I was young. So I'd say I've been to therapy for Tom several times and there's been some other stuff with my mom, but it's always been about someone else. So for me, just me, this is the first. I don't really know where to start, well, maybe I already did. I've never done cocaine. If you're wondering. Funny how that works.

DO YOU OWN ANY BINOCULARS?

Serio-Comedy:
A woman divulges a story from her past and some dark secrets involving voyeurism to a new person in her life.

So tell me something about you. Do you have any Hobbies? Do you own any binoculars? It's just something I always ask people. I do. I bought them about three months ago when I realized I was being watched in my bedroom at night, some man across the way. I saw him for the first time one night when I was undressing and talking on the phone. Fucking freak. I bet he thought I was so sexy, meanwhile, I'm on the phone with my mother going over the details of my father's wake. I remember, I just froze. I got real scared but I didn't know what to do. I didn't want to let on that I knew, in case it became worse. I just got off the phone with my mom and shut my curtains. The next day at work, I felt so pissed off, you know? Really violated and powerless. I think more, too, because I was having a private moment. I just wanted a way to make the mother fucker pay. Get my power back. So, I went and bought my very first pair of for-real, high powered binoculars, probably one of my best purchases to date. I figured, if I got his attention long enough, I could find out something about him. I knew I didn't have enough to take to the cops, so I took it upon myself to check him out. Well, it's kind of embarrassing to admit it but in the process, the whole thing actually started to turn me on. Just the idea of this stranger picking me out of everyone in the city, like some favorite channel he always turned to. I still wanted him to pay. It was very paradoxical. The thing went on for weeks. I started accidentally undressing, at approximately ten thirty, in the perfect light, every other night. Some nights, I would undress slowly and seductively like a cat on a hunt. Other nights, I would act like I couldn't stand my clothes on my body, almost ripping them off, very dramatic. One night, for a little spice, I brought a gay co-worker home and we did this whole S and M sequence. It was ridiculous but I wanted to keep him guessing. I can't believe I'm telling you this. I know it sounds sketchy but I was just as surprised as you finding out about all these secrets about myself. I actually enjoyed part of his game. I intended to confront him right away but found I was getting off on the power and control I had in knowing all along. It was like I de-powered the voyeur. After about three weeks of stripping in a variety of demeanors, fashions and moods, I decided to do my detective work. I found out everything: occupation, phone number, birthplace, favorite restaurant, social security number. Don't ask. Let's just say I have friends in all walks of life. So, I finally make this trip to Kinkos of all places. The voyeur works at Kinko's. I was expecting some Wall Street tycoon and I get paperboy. I ask to speak to the manager, Mark. Well, I say, "Nice to meet you Mark." I'm getting really pumped. Do you know what he says? "Do I know you? I say, "Sure you do. Let me refresh your memory!" I pull out my binoculars and say, "It's not very nice to spy on people, Mark. To know what they do when they're all alone. Where they sleep. How they undress." He's absolutely ghost white and everybody has stopped what they're doing. I say, "Well, I know everything about you! Everything. What's wrong Mark? Don't you like it when people pry?" That was the last time I ever saw Mark. The voyeur gave up his Muse. It was over. I think he moved shortly after the confrontation. What's scary though, about the whole experience, was not how I was violated but how I found out about parts of myself. Dark parts of myself that I would never have thought were there in a million years. I got a rush from it, from Mark. I miss him sometimes. I wonder where he is and who he's watching now. I miss the fantasy. That's what scares me. So that's a bit of me. There's more but you go ahead, you tell me something now.

RED AND BLUE

Serio-Comedy:

A woman reminisces over the turn on of being arrested, jailed and pulled over by the police.

You know there's something real comforting about the red and blue swirl of cop car lights. I realized that a long time ago, when I was taking a long drive during my trip through Colorado. It was a long night and I had been driving a long time and the cops had been chasing me for a long time too but that's neither here nor there. But I remember finally accepting the lights, you know, just surrendering. Kind of closing my eyes, making them squint so that they all blurred into one big beam, one big sort of angelic aura of protection. So, it's funny now, whenever I'm driving on the highway and I know that I'm doing something illegal. What is illegal anyway? but when I'm doing something "against the Law," There's something in me that almost craves the red and blue lights. (she pretends to be a siren) Weeooww-Weeooww! I mean, I know shouldn't crave that because, hey, my day will get slowed down, traffic will be inevitably affected but let's just say that I'm not afraid of them anymore. There's somebody out there that cares about me enough to pull me over. Somebody out there who cares about me enough to throw some beams of light my way. "Hey lady! Slow down! As a matter of fact, pull over! You're under arrest!" I like that word - arrest. Under duress? No! You're under arrest! So, the things that happened to me that night in Colorado after the lights went on, well, they don't comfort me exactly, as they do remind me of well, the fact that this story is just an illusion because anything deeper than the fantasy, points to the reality of the three nights I spent in jail. I made some good friends, don't get me wrong, we still write but I always thought then that I had enough friends and if you don't include my sister-in-law, I had five best friends before that night and now I have nineteen. Good people. They didn't understand the comfort thing with the red and blue lights but they have their own things, you know and I don't judge them for it. I didn't feel judged those nights either. So sometimes, I just like to take long drives, down long roads and close my eyes for long periods of time and wonder if there's anyone who's gonna care enough to pull me over. Do you know what I mean?

DRAMA

ANYTHING BUT THIS

Dramatic:

A woman torn apart by the betrayal of her lover confides in a friend.

I was absolutely shattered at that point so you can imagine how I felt when he called saying, "he'd like to discuss our relationship." "What fucking relationship?" I say. "The one that was destroyed when I realized that you are a bloody whore?" I hung up. Just hung up, because I knew any conversation I would have had would have meant another six months with my therapist. What a fucking pity that I know that. I've done this so many times, I actually know the consequences of deluding myself. I'm so lonely. I wish I didn't know any better. At least then I could have some company for the next fortnight. No, I'm glad you're here. God, I'm sorry. Have you ever been so angry it physically hurts? I've tried crying to relieve it but it's too overwhelming. At this point, I just feel exhausted. My sheets still smell like him and my mum's expecting us on Sunday for dinner. Pork roast. Pork roast. He's dropped off a letter trying to explain himself. He was always so good with words, bastard. Apparently, he felt neglected. I think he felt quite horny, myself. Look, I'm not suggesting that I was perfect. Iv'e been dealing with some of my own demons, too. Anything, but this, I feel like I could have worked around. Anything, but cheating. He could have fucking killed someone and I would have forgiven him. It's sort of sick, I know. I don't know why but I feel it's the ultimate betrayal. I feel like I've been set on fire and I know if I would have stayed, it would have completely burned me to a crisp. (She shakes it off) Well then, do you want another cup of tea? I'll put the kettle on.

VISITING HOURS

Dramatic:
A woman reflects on the difficulties of visiting family behind bars and questions where her loyalties lie.

It wasn't the first time I had to be patted down in order to visit with my brother in prison. I was not okay with it but then again, I wasn't okay with a lot of the things my brother did in the name of addiction. What I realized the day I took my brother's son to visit with his dad, was that no child should have to experience that. Maybe to Billy, he was in a big castle and his dad was the king. You'd be amazed at what kids can do when they need to, same stuff that comes from imagination. The prison guard had to play make believe while making sure my four year old nephew wasn't carrying drugs or God knows what else. I'm screaming inside, wondering at this point how selfish my brother's being by wanting his son to visit him in a hellhole like this. Kids know everything. I could see the bad taste in Billy's mouth. In we go through two security doors. Welcome to the land of convicts. No skirts here please! I see Mark and give him a big hug. It's been over a year since I've seen him and he's real happy to see me, my mom, and especially his beautiful boy. I can't explain the feeling of what that's like. You see the innocence in the most corrupt bastards. You remember before they were stealing from your entire family and destroying their bodies, lying their way out of everything, shaming their way into everything. You remember how they looked at the dinner table across from you on Sunday night when they were fifteen. How excited they were with their first motorcycle. You remember the first time they fell in love. My brother truly loves his baby. I see this. I'm so angry inside for this to be happening, but in my family, you make do with what you have. We go outside where there are families visiting and picnic tables to sit at. Mark is trying to get as much dialogue in with his son as he can. I am trying to get through to Mark that his life is not over and well, my mother is just trying to get through. The talk is usually the same. What I've been up to out in California and how I can't wait for him to check out San Francisco. How his parole is looking and why his lawyer isn't doing what he said he would. Do I have a boyfriend? I want to cry but I don't want to upset my mother or Billy. And so the two hours come to an end and I've got to watch my brother try and hold his shit together to look like the father he wishes he could be. Maybe I'm too hard on him. Maybe I don't know enough about life to judge. Maybe I just wish Billy could experience my brother's presence outside of this crap and I just cover it up with cold words. It was Christmas when we visited Mark. That was the last time I was patted down. Maybe I'm the selfish one.

GUARDIAN ANGEL

Dramatic:

A young woman remembers a very special, pivotal time in her life.

Do you believe in guardian angels? When I was in the ninth grade, I used to walk down a particular dirt road to school. There was this house with these great big lush roses. So big, I wondered how they stayed up. One day, I was walking by and there was this old lady sitting out on the porch. She was humming and smiling. There was something about this woman that was real interesting. I was late for school that day, so I hurried by. Every day I'd walk by and there would be this little old lady. To tell you the truth, back then I had no interest whatsoever in old people. They scared me for some reason. So fragile, like babies, but not fresh. One Monday, I was on my way home and as I walked by, sure enough, the lady was on her front steps with a big fat rose the size of my face. She called me over and handed me the flower and asked me what my name was. I didn't have much to go home to, so I stayed and chatted for a while. She had an old picture book out and some old letters from her husband who died in World War II. Her name was Eloise. What a knockout. Even as an old lady, there was something about her eyes that could have melted mountains. School was letting out for summer, so I spent every day, for two weeks straight visiting Eloise. She told me I had big things to do in my life and that I was like a warrior princess coming out of hiding. She said she could see so many wonderful things all around me. She said she had no doubt that I would soon know what she meant. Eloise smelled just like her rose garden, not like how you think most old people smell. She started telling me that she was having dreams of her husband and how they would just dance together from the minute she fell asleep until she woke. One Saturday morning, before I went to visit Eloise, I went to the fabric store. I wanted to put green velvet ribbons in her hair to match her eyes. She had showed me a picture that was black and white and told me her dress was green velvet. When I arrived, her door was locked. Eloise always left her door unlocked for me. I got worried and crawled through the back kitchen window. I remember her house was ice cold. I walked toward her bedroom and got a lump in my throat. My heart sank, I felt sick. When I got to her room Eloise's bed was made up but not with her regular lavender sheets. It was made with white sheets. Hard and sterile, properly made by some person who gets paid to do that sort of stuff. When I saw that bed, I knew she was gone. I sat down and started crying at the sight of those medical sheets wondering who would do a thing like that. I remember, I picked my head up and saw a rose on the dresser with a note to me. "Dear precious angel, don't be sad, I've gone dancing is all." Eloise is with me always. She's my angel.

TRUST

Dramatic:

A disappointed young woman tries convincing her latest "father figure" to move on from his relationship with her mother.

No, I don't have to tell you! So don't give me that crap about how I owe you Charlie, because I don't buy it anymore. You looked after my brothers and me and for that, I will always be grateful but don't bring that up every time you want to know where my mother's spent the night. Look, you're like a father to me, but you and my mother have been over for two years now. You gotta move on and find someone who can love you the way you love them. (speaking to herself) What the hell do I know, I can't keep a steady boyfriend to save my life. She's selfish. She left my father when she was done loving him and never looked back and she did the same with you, I guess. I think she does it outta protection or something. She swore to me once that no man would ever get the better of her. I don't know if she sees men as the enemy or a threat or what, but she's made it clear that she'd rather be alone than with someone who she feels isn't there. I think she does it to them before they do it to her. She told me how her father used to be out all the time with different women and how she saw her mother suffer. It don't do me any good her always leaving. I don't think I should have had to suffer losing my dad because she was scared of losing hers. Sometimes, I think I got it all figured out but then I just hurt and there's no words for it. (she pauses) Look Charlie, it's not about you. She's seen enough, I guess, to know when to say goodbye. It makes me sad because I really liked my dad. I really liked you. (sincerely) Go home Charlie, go find someone who can trust you.

My Underwater World

Dramatic:

A woman fed-up with the regular grind of being a "cosmopolitan" gal escapes into a story of a powerful past life and chooses a new direction.

You know when you think about what you might have been in a past life? I think I was a mermaid in my past life. I swam with the dolphins and didn't need a bra or a razor. I was looked up to by my fellow creatures, respected, not feared by them. I was a goddess who was strong, sensual and intuitive. We spoke from our bellies and sang from our hearts. See, that's how I feel. How could I expect you to understand this? Could you understand what that feels like? I don't feel like I'm of this world. (trying to explain) Whenever I'm not spending time getting fixes from men or weighing my worth through the needs of other people, deluding myself into thinking something isn't right or that something is missing, I feel like that mermaid again. I feel free. I feel whole like the moon of a night when it's fully lit pulling on the ocean tide. I know it doesn't make any sense. It must be from a past life, because to feel that way and then have to turn around and go to work with these fucking heels on and stay in a cement building the entire day long, get my nails buffed and my eyebrows waxed... It's so far from my mermaid world. When I'm separated from that feeling, which is more days than I'd like to admit, I feel like that mermaid with a cut fin who speaks garbled under water. I guess what I'm really trying to say is that this isn't working out between us. I don't feel like making you wrong, it's just that something isn't right.

OLD PATTERNS DIE HARD

Dramatic:

A woman not dealing with the closure of her past decides to play "vigilante." Here she is forced to re-play the events of the evening while she is being interrogated by the police.

Look! What do you people want from me? I already told you the story twice. Why do I have to keep repeating this? I was in bed trying to go to sleep. I was just trying to go to sleep when I heard it over and over. Sammy was screaming. I was just trying to mind my own business. Where the hell were you guys then, huh? I mean really, where were you? I can hear the father going nuts, just beating the shit out of this little boy. Every crack of that belt jolted me. It jolted me back to when I would watch my baby brother crawling the walls like a little bug trying to save his soul. Every whip of the belt reminded me of my father. I rolled over and tried to pretend I didn't hear. It was just torture to me to just listen. I knew it would kill me to lay there any longer, so I just got up and went down there. Over twenty apartments in that building and I'm the only one who hears this? I didn't know what the hell I was doing but it felt like something was with me, like something was, I don't know, protecting me, like I was just gliding down to where the noise was coming from. The front door was left wide open like he had just come home and started in on him. They were in the kitchen, he's still screaming, so I go right up to them thinking that might shock him or startle him or something. The bastard can't even see me. He's in some blind rage just going at this boy. (pause) The next thing you know I've got a knife in my hand and I see Sammy climbing the walls. Climbing the walls like a bug trying to save his soul, not because he's still getting beat but because his daddy's getting stabbed. (pause) He shouldn't have had to see that. That's it. I called the ambulance and then you as soon as it was over. I guess I'm guilty but I don't regret it. If he gets to breathe and put his face in the sun another day and not have to worry about a belt coming down on it. I just wish I would have had someone do the same for me. I just wish you would have gotten there sooner. That boy would have been dead if I didn't go down there. I didn't mean to hurt anybody but he could have been dead.

THE GOVERNOR'S BALL

Dramatic:
A neglected daughter, who feels more like a trophy than family, confronts her father who is running for office.

You were the life of the party last night. Looks like everyone's falling in love with the next new governor. You know, it's funny isn't it? You spend your entire life fighting for something, something that you've experienced to be true. It's amazing how you can take that same thing and use it and twist it, make a showcase out of it for all your social groups, your so-called friends. Don't act like you don't know what I'm talking about. You know what I'm talking about. I remember you fought like hell to keep me. God, that was such an epic time for me. Years of promises. Years of promises and years of bullshit. Swearing to me that you'd never hurt me, that you'd only love me and you know what? You treat me more like a trophy on some mantel than your daughter. "Go fix your hair Trisha. Go make yourself presentable for the guest Trisha." I've seen what your idea of love is, constantly smiling on the outside while I'm ripped apart wondering where the hell my daddy went. You're the one running for office. Why the fuck should I feel like I'm in the race? No! I won't keep it down. If you had to have me so badly, why can't you get off your stupid soapbox and be real with me? Not as him, but as the father

I deserve? You were completely unrecognizable last night... honestly, you have been for years now. Why did you even bother? That would be a smart move, win the kid, win the campaign? Oh, you don't want to hear that? Well, I don't want to feel that. I'm not a puppet! I'm not a puppet and I didn't think you were either. You can do this one on your own, Mr. Governor. Give me a call when my dad wants to talk.

JACARANDA IN THE SPRING

Dramatic:
A woman who's been on the run is ready to slow down.

I moved fourteen times by the time I was seventeen. I'd love to say it was because my dad was in the military. That I was one of those army brats that got to see the world and learned four different languages. Honestly, it was a bit more complicated… a lot more complicated. He was running from the law, my dad, and we were running with him. Not the smartest thing to do but we were together. What else was there? My mom was gone. It was tough, sure, and I grew up faster than most but I try not to regret it. Do you think someone can be good and bad? Yes, he was guilty. I'll be the one to say it before you ask. A wanted man, wrong place, wrong time and definitely wrong choices. A wanted man but, I believe, a good person. I need to believe it. Finally, got caught in Texas and it's been me and my brother ever since. I remember that day, it was so hot. He was walking up to the house and, from a distance, he looked like a mirage, all the heat rising. He'd brought us purple grape soda and sandwiches and said he'd be back before dinner. That's what he's like sometimes to me now, a mirage. I like it here, especially in the spring when the Jacaranda blooms wild. Reminds me things are always growing, craving to come out and see the world. Reminds me that it's normal to feel that way. I guess after so many years of laying low, I'm still trying to figure out how to let myself blossom. You make me want to be wild like the Jacaranda, Billy. I want to put all the running behind me, I do. But it's like a bad habit, the feeling of needing to move, the restlessness, the watching my back. You deserve to know where all that comes from. You promised I could tell you anything and now I've done told you everything. I'll understand if you it scares you away. Jo Jo says, underneath it all, there's a part of all of us that wants something more solid, rooted, something you can call home. When I look at you and let myself breath deep I feel myself agreeing with Jo. That boy is smarter than I give him credit for. So, if you want me stay, I mean really stay, tell me now so I can try to start letting my roots grow deep. If not, just tell me. It sure is nice here in spring.

LIVE WITH ME

Dramatic:
Set in early 1900's. A new bride attempts to understand her husband's grief over the death of his mother.

Christopher! Christopher! Could you come here for a moment? I need to speak with you. Did you see the moon last night? It was quite a sight. So fat, it looked as if it would burst. Perhaps, it has on similar occasions and henceforth, the stars. Well, did you see it? Why can't you at least give me the courtesy of seeming interested in what I have to say? Could you at least pretend? You just stare at me as though you're not sure of who I am. I know, since she passed, since your beloved mother passed, you've not been yourself and perhaps I cannot grasp the pain that stagnates in your soul but Christopher, it's been over a year. You were my lover, my reason for a continuous smile throughout the day and now I feel I've lost you to death... but we are still alive. Please, Christopher, I will not battle with death over you. I am here, alive and real, right now. Do not lose the chance to love me while I'm alive. Live with me. If you fade away, I do not know how I could bear what might remain. We are young. Don't you see? I just want to see your cheeks flushed with the color of life again... the color of love.

TAXI!

Dramatic:

A woman needing to "get away" from everything takes a taxi ride with her creative dreamer in full bloom.

I opened my eyes and there I was, in the back seat of a cab, listening to what seemed like a marathon of Barry Manilow songs. I felt a numbness of some kind as we passed, street by street by street, watching each corner light bleed into the next. I've always liked riding in the back of a cab, like some old movie and I'm this seductive lonely character who the cab driver doesn't know. He's got a fifteen minute ride with me and all he'll see is me in his mirror, some woman in the corner looking out the window like some kid looking into a candy shop. "Hey, lady, where are you going? Lady! Lady?" Good question, I thought. If I knew that, do you think I'd be taking a cab ride at three thirty in the morning just because? I figured, with the tips I'd made that night I could go to Coney Island and back. I wanted a long cigarette. You know the kind with a black filter. I wanted the driver to just know, just telepathically know and be okay with driving all night. Maybe, I thought, he was in the same boat as me. Maybe he didn't want to talk, didn't want to go back home tonight. Maybe he just wanted to forget for a while and be free like me. I kept passing him twenty dollar bills every time he tried to look at me to speak, until at one point, he just pushed the money back. He understood. It started raining as we went over the Golden Gate Bridge and that's when I knew I wasn't alone. I rolled the windows down and let the passing raindrops dance on my thighs. That was nice. That was really nice. Then I took a deep breath and told him my address. That's all. If you want to know, if you need to know… I'm tired, maybe I'll check out Coney Island some other night.

AURORA

Dramatic:

A woman shares her memories about the loss of her father and the love that remains.

My father died when I was thirteen. He was one of those heroic types, big and strong, filled with charm. His legs were blown off when he went to be a part of that uncivilized community called war. I suppose one might say I lack humility, that I couldn't possibly know anything about the way the world operates, because if I really did, I'd have a completely different attitude toward the man my father was. To all the men, all the fathers, husbands, brothers and sons and what they stood for. I don't think half of them knew. They just did what they were told. I could have loved him just as much when he came back, even more, but he couldn't handle the change. I mean could you? I think he felt so completely isolated and ripped from the world. I remember when I was brushing his hair one day, he'd always loved that. He was in good spirits. My mother had decided to make something special for dinner. I accidentally dropped the brush, picked it up, and continued to brush his hair. When I was finished, I held up the mirror for him to see and he was… just crying. Crying because I'd picked up the brush, crying because he couldn't. I'll never forget the look in his face. Crying, without making one sound. Like they had taken all of my father and stuffed him up into the rest of what they called his body. Like he was trapped from the inside. I've never felt so helpless in my life. By the time dinner was served he'd managed to gracefully receive my mother's offerings and I thought best to go along with him, his decision to transcend his despair. You know he built me that doll house? He got all the wood from his old boat and built it from scratch. He could have been a great architect. He always managed to keep his hands soft though. He said he did it so he wouldn't scare me and mother away. He could have been a great anything. He took his life that night. He tucked me in, told me a story about aurora borealis, and how the lights came into existence, and kissed me on my left cheek. He didn't do it in the house. He went to the shed. He used to love being out there. When I was seventeen, I moved to Alaska. It was like nothing I'd ever known. I found the lights and decided to stay for a while. Watching, transcending my despair. Aurora borealis. It felt like he was there. And then, well, then, here I am. Ten or so years in between, but... here I am.

Dramatic:

A woman shattered by the memory of seeing the destructive ways of her parents, taps into her deep fear of relationships.

I remember it, but more like it was a story told to me. I couldn't have been more than four or five years old. My mother looked like she was possessed. She had pulled a gun on my father. It was at the top of the stairs, my mother was standing in front of the bathroom door. I can't imagine where I would have been standing, but I remember. I also can't imagine her doing that in front of me, but then again, I can't imagine her doing a lot of the things she did in front of me. I remember the gun was a really muted silver thing pointing at my dad. I sensed that my mom felt helpless, like she was doing only what she thought she could do, like she had no choice. It is sick that, to this day, I have this vision embedded in my head. A little girl doesn't need to see her mother trying to kill her daddy. I don't know what was more painful, my mother doing that or my father laughing at her with the barrel of a gun pointing towards his face. Laughing? The whole thing was, and always will be, twisted. He was laughing because he had the bullets. To see my mother's face, knowing that she had finally hit bottom, pulled a gun on her husband, to be laughed at in her face? It doesn't get much more powerless than that. He was probably shitting his pants and only laughing out of sheer desperation, some pathetic attempt to regain her power in front of someone who had obviously lost their mind. The whole thing makes me want to puke. What the fuck kind of message is that to a little kid? I'll tell you what…

Mommy trying to destroy daddy.

Mommy getting humiliated.

Daddy laughing at his own death.

If a gun can't do it…

She will always be helpless.

I hate that word. Helpless.

I think I'm going to hold off on having children for a while. Yeah, that's probably a good idea.

You Want My Job

Dramatic:
A tough, no nonsense editor sheds some light on a younger journalist after she almost jeopardizes a top story.

It looks like I've hired myself a good old-fashioned liar. You are a liar. You can sit here and tell me that you did not lie and again, you'll be lying. Withholding and distorting the truth, as you know it, is lying. They may call that "being nice" from your neck of the woods, sweetheart, but if you work for me and plan on growing in this company, and for that matter anywhere in this fucking town, I expect nothing but complete honesty. What exactly didn't you understand about the word accountability when I gave you your job? I told you, when I hired you, that it wasn't going to be easy. I also told you, that within a few years, you could be one of the top journalists in this city. While, I realize you were trying to save my feelings from being hurt and I appreciate your considering how those comments may have come across, you need to understand that this is not the Mary Tyler Moore Show. There are no 30-second commercials breaks here. If you have any information for me, any at all, make sure I get it. Period. I've learned in a very short amount of time to take what's under this skirt and in this brain and prove to every one of those ignorant pricks that I know precisely what I'm doing. Look, you're a smart girl. I like you.

You wouldn't be standing here if I didn't but it's time you woke up. You came this close to losing that story. You want my job. That's what I want you to want. That's how I want you think. Now go in there and get us that story or don't bother coming back. Get every bit of information and save the nicey nice for someone else. (she pages her secretary on the phone) Maureen, get me Jake Ashton. (re: back to her target) I like that red lipstick on you...very flattering. Don't look so down, everything is going to be just fine.

WELCOME TO THE WORLD KID

Dramatic:

A woman sits at a bus stop grieving her recently deceased father.

It occurred to me on Friday, today, that it has been two weeks since my father died. A fortnight. Fourteen days. Seven times two. The numbers feel like they keep falling out of my head like a box full of LEGOS being dumped into a black hole. None of the things that they suggest will prepare the living have an ounce of real weight... more like a featherweight joke. I know he was old. I know everyone's day comes, and in my case, fortunately, we said the "I love you's" and the "there's nothing to forgive" business. But no matter how much time you take to complete things, it's not some package with a pretty bow. It's pathetic and honestly, I feel like the brunt of a very cruel, very holier-than-thou joke. I saw his face in mine, in the lines, the ones on the side of his mouth. Fucking charmer. When he was in his last days, we all stood over his body he was like a newborn child, helpless but in good hands. We got to be alone together a few times, in the silence and, for a moment or two, I felt my breath was his, like I was somehow possessed by my need for him. Like we had our own eyes but we were the same entity. Even now, I taste his lingering DNA. I've missed my bus and it will take another twenty minutes for the next. Must have gone temporarily blind and deaf as my bus pulled up and pulled away right in front of me without my knowledge. My sister Maureen will be worried. She's probably pacing up and down the front steps like a retiree in training. She will scold me for not having my cell… for having no juice in my cell. I will let her go at me and I may even say something insensitive so she really lets me have it. That will feel good for both of us. A little relief maybe. I hope she hits me. Maureen is my younger-older sister. What can I say? I was the learning curve child, the one they would learn on and she was the one they'd curve to. Sure, death brings you closer to one another but what's the point of being close when you're numb? So when you thaw out you have someone who's there for you. Jesus, this is ridiculous. I wonder how I looked to the last bus. Like I was on dope or a schizophrenic maybe? I was sitting next to a girl that, go figure, reminded me of myself at her age. She was blowing big bubbles of bright, hot pink gum and I wanted to just pop one, just one. She was twelve, maybe thirteen. She had little growing boobies and seemed anxious and excited at the same time like she just, just wanted to fly. My father always warned me about flying, as if the higher I went, the harder I would fall. The truth is, we all fall anyway, so we ought to go as high as we can while we have the wherewithal, the chutzpa He was a hypocrite, an open one, mind you. "Yeah I know, I'm a walking contradiction. Welcome to the world kid." Yeah… welcome to the world.

To Consider

I've deleted a lot of "notes" within the body of monologues. Beats here, pauses there, dialects, the list goes on. You know what's up. My suggestion would be to just give theses pieces several read-throughs before you committ to anything. Keep finding it. It's there, in the text, or lack thereof. This is not correct, it's human. The way people speak suggests so much more than what they are actually saying. Now, fully go for it with your one of a kind self... and have a ball.

TELL IT LIKE IT IS

_____

_____

_____

_____

_____

_____

_____

_____

_____

_____

_____

_____

_____

_____

_____

_____

_____

_____

_____

_____

_____

_____

REMINISCE

_____

_____

_____

_____

_____

_____

_____

_____

_____

_____

_____

_____

_____

_____

_____

_____

_____

_____

_____

_____

_____

_____

WORK IT OUT

LOCK IT IN

PROCESS

OH THE JOY!

Made in the USA
Lexington, KY
03 April 2019